Moments for Marvelous Mothers

Written by
Robert J. Strand

ORDERING INFORMATION
Individual sales can be had at selected bookstores or you can order direct from Rojon, Inc. at P.O. Box 3898, Springfield, MO 65808-3898 or call our customer service number, 918-459-2106.
Quantity sales are available at special discounts on bulk purchases by corporations, associations, churches and others. For details, contact Rojon Inc. at the above address.
Orders by trade bookstores and wholesalers can be made through the above address as well.

ISBN: 0-9717039-0-6

First printing: January 2002

All Scripture references are from **"The New King James Version"** (Thomas Nelson Publishers) unless otherwise noted.

Design by Marc Mcbride

ROJON PUBLISHING
P. O. Box 3898
Springfield, MO 65808-3898
Fax: 417-883-0556

Presented to:

Patricia Annette Hockman

Presented by:

Church of the Lakes

Date:

_5 – 12 – 2002_

Dedication:

To the mothers in my life who have given me my understanding and insight into motherhood. They are my mother, Ruth; spouse, Donna; daughter, Cheriee; and daughters-in-law, Becky and Jennifer. These are all "Strand" mothers.
Thank you for the life lessons.

Contents

Love

SEVERAL YEARS AGO in a tropical country where many Americans were living, a terrifying eye disease struck. It affected primarily children. American children were more vulnerable because of a deficiency in their immune systems. The signs were unmistakable. Five days after the first symptoms appeared the child would begin to go blind. Parents were understandably terrified.

One morning...one of the American mothers awoke to see all the symptoms of this disease in her little girl's eyes. She immediately took her to the doctor only to be told that there was no hope!

Holding back the tears, the mother then took her daughter by the hand and walked her to a nearby field. This mother picked up her child and held her. Again and again she told her to notice the sunlight and how it lit the landscape.

Then they knelt among the yellow wild flowers. The mother picked one, smelled its aroma with her daughter and carefully examined the lovely, complicated structure that only God could make.

She then held her little girl up to her face. "Look at me," she commanded gently. "What color is my hair?"

"Black, Mommy. Black and pretty."

"And my eyes...look at them. What color are they?"

"Blue, blue like the sky," she said, patting her mother's face with a childish affection.

The mother then held her close, looked into her daughter's eyes, "Now, sweetheart, what do you see in your mother's eyes?"

"Love, Mommy. I see love!"

(Virgil Hensley, adapted from a fund raising letter)

LOVE IS MORE
Some think that love is all flowers and good times
but I think that love is more than just that…
Love is the bad as well as the better,
not lived alone but a journey together.
Something that only the closest can share,
with communication, respect and delicate care.

As a mother comforts her child, so will I comfort you;
and you will be comforted…
(Isaiah 66:13, NIV)

Mikey's Goal

LAST NIGHT was the last soccer game for my eight-year-old son's soccer team. It was the final quarter. The score was 2 to 1 with my son's team in the lead. Parents shouted encouragement from the sidelines as the boys clashed on the field.

With less than ten seconds remaining, the ball rolled in front of my son's team-mate, one Mikey O'Donnel. With shouts of "Kick IT!" echoing across the field, Mikey reared back and gave it everything he had. All around me the crowd fell silent as the ball flew into the goal. Mikey O'Donnel had scored!

Mikey had scored all right...but in the wrong goal, ending the game in a tie! For a moment there was total silence in the crowd as well as on the field. You see Mikey has "Down's Syndrome" and for him there is no such thing as a wrong goal. All goals were celebrated by a joyous hug from Mikey. He had even been known to hug the opposing players when they scored.

The silence was broken when Mikey, his face filled with joy, grabbed my son, hugged him and yelled, "I scored! I SCORED! Everybody won! EVERYBODY WON!" For a long moment I held my breath, not sure how my son would react. I need not have worried. I watched through tears, as my son threw up his hand in the classic high-five salute and started chanting, "Way to go, Mikey! Way to go, Mikey!"

Within moments both teams surrounded Mikey joining in the chant and con-gratulating him on his first goal of the season! Later that night, when my daughter asked who had won the match, my son smiled and replied, "It was a tie. Everybody won!"

MEASURING MORAL QUALITY

As water cannot rise higher than its source, so the moral quality in an act can never be higher than the motive that inspires it.

(A. W. Tozer)

The LORD our God, the LORD is one!
You shall love the LORD your God with all your heart, with all your soul, and with all your strength. And these words which I command you today shall be in your heart.
You shall teach them diligently to your children, and shall talk of them when you sit in your house, when you walk by the way, when you lie down, and when you rise up.
(Deuteronomy 6:4-7)

9

How to Spell...

KERRY SETLER tells us the following story: My mom and I were eating lunch at one of the many fast-food restaurants in our town. A small boy near us hopped down from where he sat with his mother. He ran to drop the remains of his dinner through the swinging lid of a trash can. Rather than returning to his seat, the boy stood there for nearly a minute, his eyes fixed directly ahead. His lips were moving in silent reading until he abruptly snapped out of his trance and raced back to his mother.

"Mom," he said, pulling at her coat. "Mom!"

She looked down, still eating and mumbled, "Hmmmm?"

"I know how to spell garbage!"

"Oh?" She dabbed at the corner of her mouth with a napkin. "How do you spell garbage?"

This little guy straightened his spine until he stood at perfect cub-scout attention and announced clearly, "P-U-S-(ahhh)-H and that spells garbage." He waited for his mother's response.

In seconds the mother flashed a smile back at her son and reached out, drawing him tightly to her. She kissed him and whispered, "I L-O-V-E you. Know what that spells?" She paused, he looked at her, and she continued, "That spells what I feel for you!"

What a wonderful moment caught in time! These are the moments for which God created mothers! What kind of an impact will that moment have on that particular little boy for time as well as for eternity?

PATIENCE AND RELATIONSHIPS
Patience with others is Love.
Patience with self is Hope.
Patience with God is Faith.
(Adel Bestavros)

Love suffers long and is kind; love does not envy; love does not parade itself, is not puffed up; does not behave rudely, does not seek its own, is not provoked, thinks no evil; does not rejoice in iniquity, but rejoices in the truth; bears all things, believes all things, hopes all things, endures all things.
LOVE NEVER FAILS!
(I Corinthians 13:4-8a)

The Life Worth the Fight

Oh, it's just the little homely things,
*   The unobtrusive friendly things,*
The "Won't-you-let-me-help-you" things
*   That make our pathway light.*
The "Laugh-with-me-it's funny" things,
*   And it's the jolly, joking things,*
The "Never-mind-the-trouble" things
*   That make the world seem bright.*

For the countless famous things
The wondrous, record-breaking things,
These "Never-can-be-equaled" things
*   That all the papers cite,*
Are not the little human things,
The "everyday-encountered" things,
The "Just-because-I-like-you" things,
*   That make us quite happy.*

*   So here's to all the little things,*
The "Done-and-then-forgotten" things,
Those "Oh-it's-simply-nothing" things
*   That make life worth the fight!*

(Author is unknown)

Grandmother and Granddaughter

GRANDMOTHER AND GRANDDAUGHTER, a precocious ten-year-old, were spending the evening together when the little girl suddenly looked up and asked, "How old are you, Grandma?"

The grandmother was a bit startled, but knowing her granddaughter's quick little mind, wasn't shocked. "Well, honey…when you are my age you don't share your age with anybody."

"Awww, go ahead, Grandma…you can trust me!"

"No dear, I never tell my age."

Grandma then got busy fixing supper and suddenly realized the little darling had been absent for about twenty minutes…much too long! She checked and found her upstairs in her bedroom. Granddaughter had dumped all the contents of her purse on the top of her bed and was sitting in the middle of the mess holding her grandmother's driver's license.

When their eyes met, the child announced, "Grandma, you're seventy-six!"

"Why, yes, I am. How did you know that?"

"I found the date of your birthday here on your driver's license and subtracted that year from this year…so, you're seventy-six!"

"That's right, sweetheart. Your grandmother is seventy-six."

The little girl continued, staring at the driver's license and added, "You also made an 'F' in sex, Grandma!"

Kids…aren't they just delightful? Can you remember a time when your life was more joyful than now? Kids laugh an average of 150 times a day, adults about 10. What's happened to us? Somewhere between childhood innocence and now, life has become too grim! And besides, who says that being a Christian means a long face? It's time to laugh more!

The writer Balzac called life, with all of its tragedies and twists, a human comedy. There is a lot in life that seems unfair, but seeing the absurdity, finding something to laugh at makes it easier to endure and certainly a lot more fun. It also combats illness!

(Bernie S. Siegel, M.D.)

He who sits in the heavens shall laugh…
(Psalm 2:4)

Mothers

MOTHERS come in various sizes: skinny, just right, filled out and "oops!" They are found everywhere: in maternity wards, over ironing boards, teaching three-year-olds how to sing "Jesus Loves Me," at the grocery store, on the job, up and around while the rest of the family is down with the flu, championing causes, turning the right out of the left, kissing where it hurts, perspiring over new math, changing her husband's mind, looking daggers at the umpire who has just called her child out on strikes, popping corn at the school festival, on her knees with an open Bible, taking away privileges, pushing piano practice, organizing the family day, saving for a special vacation and sitting in the front pew while her child is being married.

A MOTHER IS happiness with tears in her eyes,

Love with firm paddle in hand,

Joy watching Dad and the kids hungrily devour chicken and noodles so they can get to the dessert,

Sacrifice eating the neck and wings and leaving the plump breast and drum sticks,

Foresight stashing away every bit of extra for college,

Faith singing in the choir, herding primaries, serving another church supper, keeping up the pledge, making a call on a shut-in and sending a box to the missionaries.

BEING A MOTHER is such a demanding task that God has entrusted it only to females. There is no experience in life so costly, so rewarding, so aging, and so exciting as being a **MOTHER!**

The only thing of value we can give kids is what we are, not what we have.

(Leo Buscaglia)

Many daughters have done well,
But you excel them all.
Charm is deceitful and beauty is passing,
But a woman who fears the LORD, she shall be praised.
Give her of the fruit of her hands,
AND let her own works praise her in the gates.
(Proverbs 31:29-31)

The Real Son

LEO TOLSTOY often told old folk stories to challenge his listeners. One of his favorites is about an aged man who happened to overhear the conversations of three village peasant women drawing water at the communal well.

The first one to speak described her son in the most glowing terms... he was an entertainer! And what an entertainer he was, he surpassed all the others with his dexterity, skill, presentation and ability to hold an audience.

The second of these three mothers, not to be outdone, extolled her son's beautiful voice! With his wonderful tenor voice he could thrill the young and the old, create happy and sad moods in his listeners with notes as sweet as the song of a nightingale.

Then the two turned to the third mother and asked, "In what kind of talent does your son excel?"

The third mother simply replied, "My son is quite an ordinary boy who has no special gifts or talents of which I can report."

The old man then followed the three mothers on their way back to the village. Each carried two heavy buckets of water which made them stop for a rest. As they rested, their three sons came running to meet them. The first one turned one handspring followed by a somersault all the way down the path toward his mother. The women stood admiring the young entertainer. The second son came toward his mother singing like a nightingale. His singing moved the mothers, each wiped away a tear because they were so moved. The third son just ran to his mother, picked up the heavy buckets she had been carrying and he lugged them all the way home for her.

Then the three women inquired of the old man, "What do you have to say about our sons?"

"Your sons?" responded the astonished man, "I saw only one son. I recognized only one real son."

THE BOOK OUR MOTHERS READ

We search the world for truth; we cull
The good, the pure, the beautiful,
From graven stone and written scroll,
And all old flower-fields of the soul;
And, weary seekers of the best,
We come back laden from the quest,
To find that all the sages said
Is in the BOOK our mothers read.

(John Greenleaf Whittier)

My son (and daughter), keep your father's command, And do not forsake
the law of your mother. Bind them continually upon your heart;
Tie them around your neck.
When you roam, they will lead you;
When you sleep, they will keep you;
And when you awake, they will speak with you.
For the commandment is a lamp,
And the law a light;
Reproofs of instruction are the way of life.
(Proverbs 6:20-23)

The Final Goodbye

SHE WAS SPECIAL! She was one of those wonderful, old saints who was there every time the church doors were open…never any excuses. Salt of the earth, faithful. During the weekdays she busied herself with Christian duties and simple dedication. She had been a widow for more than a decade. She had been struggling with a fatal disease for months, in fact, she had been dying for months and she was fully prepared to do so.

The Rev. Kirk Niemeyer, her pastor, stopped by quite often to visit. So he was understandably puzzled to receive her message requesting a special visit from the pastor.

He called on her that very evening. She was in excellent spirits. "Kirk," she said, "we both know that this can't go on much longer. When I die, I want you to promise me that you will carry out a request of mine."

"Of course," Pastor Niemeyer promised her.

She reinforced the promise, "Kirk, you do it. I'm sure my kids wouldn't do it." Again he assured her.

She then explained her request. "When my casket is opened at the funeral and all my friends come by for a last look, I want them to see me ready to be buried with a table fork in my right hand." Niemeyer seemed more than a bit puzzled by her request. She continued, "I want you to tell this to the congregation: You know what it means when they clear the dishes from a big meal and someone says, 'keep your fork.' You know that something good is coming…maybe a piece of warm apple pie with cheese on it or a big slab of chocolate cake."

She concluded, "Keep your fork, means something good is coming. Kirk, I want to be buried with a dessert fork in my hand. It will be my way of saying, 'The best is yet to come'!"

Ten days later, she was buried with a fork in her right hand just as she had requested. Everyone who saw her in the casket saw her final witness. For her, death was not a disaster…it was dessert!

Life is short and life is not always fair! But it's long enough so that you can prepare for the day and time when you will be saying a final goodbye. Will you be saying your last goodbye with a dessert fork in hand?

Precious in the sight of the LORD
Is the death of His saints!
(Psalm 116:15)

The Favorite Child

EVERY MOTHER HAS A FAVORITE CHILD! Really? You don't believe that? Read on. After all, she is only a human mother. Okay, the favorite child is the one for whom she shall feel a special, motherly closeness. It is to this child that a love is offered that nobody else could possibly understand at that "particular" moment in one of life's hard times.

NOW... read on as you can hear mothers everywhere begin to respond...

MY FAVORITE child was born with a cleft lip and couldn't take milk from a bottle without filling his little tummy with air. He had colic all the time...and later, he always seemed to be the one needing stitches in his head.

MY FAVORITE child is the one who broke her arm while climbing a tree on the very first day of her summer vacation. WHO was sick with mumps during Christmas. WHO was so sick at her 13th birthday party she couldn't eat any of her favorite chocolate cake and had to watch all her invited friends gorge themselves.

MY FAVORITE child was the one who was passed over and chosen last for school games. WHO never quite made the grades that an older sibling had achieved. WHO happened to see the family pet dog struck down by a car on the highway.

MY FAVORITE child had to wear a protective helmet to bed to protect the head injury from further injury. WHO had a teacher who made life miserable for him in the fourth grade. WHO I held in my arms all the way to the emergency room so more stitches could be set. WHO struggled with asthma.

MY FAVORITE child spent Christmas Eve away from the family for the first time because he forgot to put gas into the tank and was stranded alone between college and home. WHO, on the first date couldn't get the car started in the fast-food parking lot where he'd taken her to eat following the ball game. WHO had his first bike stolen because he left it out.

MY FAVORITE child is the one who forgot all those carefully learned lines for the church school special Easter program. WHO lost the money so lovingly earned and saved in order to buy a favorite doll. WHO really messed up at the piano recital in front of all those people.

MY FAVORITE child, who at her big moment as a cheerleader, fell flat on her face! WHO was cut from the softball team. WHO failed the most important ritual of passage, a driver's license exam.

MY FAVORITE child dropped what would have been the winning touchdown pass in the end-zone.

MY FAVORITE child is the one whom I disciplined for cheating. WHOM I also grounded in front a friend who happened to be visiting. WHOM I told had been a royal mess-up in the family. WHOM I over-reacted to.

MY FAVORITE child slammed doors in frustrated anger because of the way she had been treated by her "best" friend. WHO cried when she was ignored by the "in" people in her high school. WHO withdrew and refused to talk about it.

MY FAVORITE child always looked unkempt no matter what he put on. WHO had a big date with the most wonderful girl in the world and his car broke down on that Saturday night and they walked back home.

MY FAVORITE child struggled with a bad temper that seemed to blow at the most inopportune times. WHO couldn't decide what to do in life. WHO was the 96th student when the first 95 had been chosen for medical school. WHO was jilted by the love of a short life.

ALL MOTHERS EVERYWHERE HAVE THEIR FAVORITE CHILD! And it seems to always be the same one! THE ONE WHO NEEDS YOU AT A CRITICAL LIFE MOMENT!

That "one" who needs you at the moment may be frustrated, hurt, happy, depressed, injured, rejected, self-centered, immature, selfish, disappointed, lonely, questioning, hungry, wondering, helpless, in love, misguided…or, what-have-you.

This favorite child may need you to hold on to…to scream at…to verbally attack…to hug…to dump on…to cry with…to encourage…to love…to vent…to use your credit card…to question…to phone.

But perhaps, more than anything else, **MY FAVORITE CHILD** simply needs a mother just to be there!

If I Had My Life...

If I had my life to live over again, I'd try to make more mistakes next time.

I would relax, I would limber up, I would be sillier than I have been this trip.

I know of very few things I would take seriously.

I would take more trips. I would be crazier.

I would climb more mountains, swim more rivers, and watch more sunsets.

I would do more walking and looking.

I would eat more ice cream and less beans.

I would have more actual troubles and fewer imaginary ones.

You see, I'm one of those people who lives life prophylactically and sensibly, hour after hour, day after day. Oh, I've had my moments and if I had to do it over again I'd have more of them.

In fact, I'd try to have nothing else, just moments, one after another, instead of living so many years ahead each day. I've been one of those people who never goes anywhere without a thermometer, a hot-water bottle, a gargle, a raincoat, aspirin and a parachute.

If I had to do it over again I would go places, do things and travel lighter than I have.

If I had my life to live over I would start barefooted earlier in the spring and stay that way later in the fall.

I would play hookey more. I wouldn't make such good grades, except by accident. I would ride on more merry-go-rounds. I'd pick more daisies!

(Brother Jeremiah)

Respect

DURING THE AMERICAN REVOLUTION, an officer of the Continental Army was sent around through the Virginia countryside to confiscate horses for military use.

This was a very normal military practice in those days. When the army had a need, they would ask for donations. If these were not forthcoming, they confiscated the needed items, using the rights of eminent domain.

This particular officer approached a fine old southern mansion, rang the bell and asked to speak to the owner. A dignified elderly lady appeared and he was invited into the parlor. He came directly to the point of this visit, "Madam, I am claiming your horses on orders from my Commander."

"Sir," she answered, "you cannot have my horses! I need them now for spring plowing and planting. Who is your Commander?"

He, in full military dress, pulled himself to full attention, replied, "General George Washington, Commander of the American Army."

"You go back and tell General George Washington that his mother says he cannot have any of her horses," she replied firmly but with a slight smile!

Now wouldn't you have loved to have been there to take in the scene as this officer came back to their camp with this report to the General?!? I love it! Don't you wonder what the Commander must have thought and said? And you can be assured that this tidbit of news must have traveled like wildfire through that military outpost! Mom said, "NO!"

Mother…it is important that you say "no," mean "no," practice "no," enforce your "no," and live by "no."

*All I am I owe to my mother… I attribute all my success
in life to the moral, intellectual, and physical education
I received from her.*

(George Washington)

**Train up a child
in the way he should go.
And when he is old
he will not depart from it.
(Proverbs 22:6)**

A Strange Answer to Prayer

A MOTHER was at work when she received a phone call that her daughter was very sick with a fever. She left work and stopped by the pharmacy to get some medication for her daughter.

When returning to her car she found it locked with the keys still in the ignition. She was in a desperate hurry to get home and now didn't know what to do. She called home and told the baby sitter what had happened.

The baby sitter told her the daughter was getting worse. She also told her to use a coat hanger to open the door. The mother looked around and found an old rusty coat hanger on the ground, possibly left by someone else who had locked their keys in the car.

Then...she looked at the hanger and said, "I don't know how to use this." So she bowed her head and asked God for help.

Within less than five minutes an old rusted out car pulled up with a dirty, greasy, bearded man who was wearing an old biker skull rag on his head and a leather jacket. The woman thought, *"Just great, God. This is what you have sent to help me?"*

But...she was desperate, so she decided to be grateful, though nervous. The man got out and asked if he could help her. She said, "Yes, my daughter is very sick. I stopped to get her some medication and I locked my keys in the car. I just have to get home. Please, can you use this hanger to unlock my car?"

He took the hanger and in about thirty seconds he had the car open. The lady hugged the man and through tears said, "Thank you so much. You are a very nice man."

He responded, "Lady, I am not a nice man; I've just spent the last few years in prison for car theft. In fact, I was just released this morning."

The woman hugged the man again and with tears of gratitude, said, "Thank you, God, for sending me a professional!"

"Power is of two kinds. One is obtained by the fear of punishment and the other by the art of love. Power based on love is a thousand times more effective and permanent than the one derived by the fear of punishment."
(Mohandas Ghandi)

"For the mountains shall depart and the hills be removed, but My kindness shall not depart from you, nor shall My covenant of peace be removed," says the LORD, who has mercy on you.
(Isaiah 54:10)

Two Versions of Going to Bed

MOM AND DAD were watching TV when Mom said, "I'm tired and it's getting late. I think I'll go to bed."

SHE went to the kitchen to make sandwiches for the next day's lunches, rinsed out the popcorn bowls, took meat out of the freezer for dinner the following evening, checked the cereal box levels, filled the sugar container, put spoons and bowls on the table and set the timer on the coffee pot for brewing the next morning.

SHE then put some wet clothes in the dryer, put a load of clothes into the washer, ironed a shirt and sewed on a loose button. She picked up the newspapers strewn on the floor, picked up the game pieces left on the table and put the telephone book back into the drawer. She watered the plants, emptied a wastebasket and hung up a towel to dry. She yawned and stretched and headed for the bedroom.

SHE stopped by the desk and wrote a note to the teacher, counted out some cash for the field trip and pulled a textbook out from hiding under the chair. She signed a birthday card for a friend, addressed and stamped the envelope and wrote a quick list for the grocery store. She put both near her purse. Mom then washed her face, put on moisturizer, brushed and flossed her teeth and trimmed her nails.

Hubby called, "I thought you were going to bed."

"I'm on my way," she said.

SHE put some water into the dog's dish and put the cat outside, then made sure the doors were locked. She looked in on each of the kids and turned out a bedside lamp, hung up a shirt, threw some dirty socks in to the hamper and had a brief conversation with the one up still doing homework. In her own room, she set the alarm, laid out clothing for the next day, straightened up the shoe rack. She added three things to her list of things to do for tomorrow.

HUBBY, about that time, turned off the TV and announced to no one in particular, "I'm going to bed," and he did!

(Karen Mallory)

*Countless times each day a mother does what no
one else can do quite as well.
She wipes away a tear; whispers a word of hope,
eases a child's fears. She teaches, ministers, loves, and
nurtures the next generation of citizens.
And she challenges and cajoles her kids to do their
best and be the best. But no editorials praise these
accomplishments…where is the coverage
our mothers rightfully deserve?*

(James Dobson & Gary Bauer)

She watches over the ways of her household,
And does not eat the bread of idleness.
Her children rise up
and call her blessed;
Her husband also, and he
praises her.
(Proverbs 31:27-28)

Common Sense Passes Away

TODAY WE MOURN the passing away of a mother's good and long time friend by the name of "Common Sense."

Common Sense lived a long life but recently died from heart failure at the beginning of the new millennium. No one really knows how old she was since her birth records were long ago lost in bureaucratic red tape.

She selflessly devoted her life to service in homes, schools, hospitals, factories and offices, helping folks get jobs done without fanfare and senseless foolishness.

For decades, petty rules, silly laws and frivolous lawsuits held no power over Common Sense. She was credited with cultivating such valued lessons as knowing when to come in out of the rain, the early bird gets the worm, eat your supper, put on your mittens and life isn't always fair. And, when something hits the fan, it never gets distributed equally.

Common Sense lived by simple, sound financial policies (don't spend more than you earn), reliable parenting strategies (adults are in charge, not kids), and it's okay to come in second (also known as the some one always loses rule).

A veteran of the Industrial Revolution, the Great Depression and the Technological Revolution, Common Sense survived cultural and educational trends including feminism, body piercing, whole language and new math.

But her health declined when she became infected with the "if-it-only-helps-one-person-it's-worth-it" virus. In recent years her waning strength proved no match for the ravages of overbearing federal regulation such as the "one objection overrules the majority" rule.

She watched in pain as good people became ruled by self-seeking lawyers and enlightened auditors. Her health rapidly deteriorated when schools endlessly implemented zero tolerance policies, reports of a six-year-old charged with sexual harassment for kissing a classmate, a teen suspended for taking a swig of mouthwash after lunch and a teacher fired for reprimanding an unruly student.

It declined even further when schools had to get parental consent to administer aspirin to a student but cannot inform the parent when the female student is pregnant or wants an abortion.

One of the last coffin nails was protecting the criminal's rights while ignoring those of the victims.

Finally, Common Sense lost her will to live as the Ten Commandments became contraband, churches became businesses, criminals received better treatment than victims and federal judges stuck their noses in everything from Boy Scouts to professional sports, while staying far away from all matters having to do with politicians.

As the end neared, Common Sense drifted in and out of logic but was kept informed of developments regarding questionable regulations for asbestos, low flow toilets, smart guns, global warming, speckled owls, the nurturing of prohibition laws and mandatory air bags.

Finally when told that the homeowners association restricted exterior furniture only to that which enhanced property values…she breathed her last.

Common Sense was preceded in death by her parents, Truth and Trust; her husband, Discretion; her daughter, Responsibility; and her son, Reason.

She is survived by three step-brothers: Rights, Tolerance, and Whiner.

Not many attended her funeral because so few realized she was gone. It was too late…or is it? Will the mothers in our land resurrect her once more to be the guiding direction in life? Will she be taught at mother's knee once more?

Common Sense…the knack of seeing things as they are, and doing things as they ought to be done.

(C. E. Stone)

Keep my words, And treasure my commands within you. Keep my commands and live, And my law as the apple of your eye. Bind them on your fingers; write them on the tablet of your heart. Say to wisdom, "You are my sister."

(Proverbs 7:1-4)

How I Survived

CAROL'S HUSBAND was killed in an accident last year. Jim, only fifty-two, was driving home from work. The other driver was a teenager with a high blood-alcohol level. Jim died instantly at impact. The teen was in the emergency room less than two hours and then released to go home.

There were other ironic twists: It was Carol's fiftieth birthday and Jim had two plane tickets to Hawaii in his pocket. He was going to surprise her. Instead, he was killed by a drunk driver.

Time passed…almost a year when a good friend, Debby finally asked, "Carol, how have you survived all of this?"

Her eyes welled up with tears. Debby immediately thought she had said the wrong thing…but Carol gently took Debby's hand and said, "It's all right, Debby."

Then she continued after the pause, "I want to tell you… the day I married Jim, I also promised I would never let him leave the house in the morning without telling him I love him. He made the same promise. It got to be a joke between us and as babies came along, it got to be a hard promise to keep. I remember running down the drive-way, saying, 'I love you,' through clenched teeth when I was mad. And sometimes driving to the office to put a note in his car or under the wipers. It was like a funny challenge.

"We made a lot of memories trying to say, 'I love you' before noon every day of our married life.

"The morning Jim died, he left a birthday card in the kitchen and slipped out to the car. I heard the engine starting. 'Oh, no, you don't buster, I thought.' I raced out and banged on the car window until he rolled it down. Then I said, 'Here on my fiftieth birthday, Mr. James E. Bennett, I Carol Bennett, go on record as saying I love you!'

"That's how I've survived, Debby. Knowing that the last words I said to Jim were, 'I love you'!"

If you love someone…how about telling them, NOW?! If you have to, call them long distance, drive to the office or shop, rent a billboard, hire a skywriter, send a fax, write an e-mail, write a letter…but just tell them! Tell them NOW!

Do not withhold good from those to whom it is due,
When it is in the power of your hand to do so!
(Proverbs 3:27)

Persistence

PERHAPS you have read one or more of the books of Peter and Barbara Jenkins: *Walk Across America* and *The Walk West: A Walk Across America 2*. If you haven't, you should read them. They are interesting true life odysseys and both are wonderful.

Peter walked by himself with his dog from New York state to New Orleans. There he met his future wife, Barbara, and together they took up the trek heading northwest across Texas, New Mexico, Idaho, Utah and across Oregon to the Pacific Ocean.

When they were near the end of their trek they wrote to many of the people who had befriended them along the way to meet them in Florence, Oregon to walk the last mile with them and celebrate the completion of their remarkable journey. One of those who joined them was Barbara's eighty-three-year-old grandmother. She led them and she was singing as she did so. Let's read the paragraph from the book:

"Her voice was squeaky and high but sounded sweet to me as the slapping ocean waves that were just over the ridge ahead of us. Grandma's eighty-three-year-old hands were wrinkled, little and frail, but she held to us with a tight grip, walking in brisk steps. She wasn't even five feet tall and weighed a light eighty-five pounds but her tiny steps led the way, setting the pace for all of our friends behind us."

As they came over the dunes Barbara's grandma led them in singing the old church hymn, *"The Last Mile of the Way:"*

> *If I walk in the pathway of duty,*
> *If I work till the close of the day,*
> *I shall see the great King in His beauty*
> *When I've gone the last mile of the way.*

We rate ability in people by what they finish...
not by what they begin!

THEREFORE we also, since we are surrounded by so great a cloud of
witnesses, let us lay aside every weight and the sin which so easily
ensnares us, and let us run with endurance the race that
is set before us,
Looking unto Jesus, the author and finisher of our faith,
Who for the joy that was set before Him endured the cross, despising
the shame, and has sat down at the right hand of the throne of God.
For consider Him who endured...
(Hebrews 12:1-3a)

Today I Can

Today I can complain about my health,
OR
I can celebrate being alive.

Today I can moan that it is raining,
OR
Be joyful at all that grows from rain.

Today I can regret all I don't have,
OR
Rejoice in everything I do.

Today I can mourn everything I have lost,
OR
Eagerly anticipate what's to come.

Today I can complain that I have to work,
OR
Celebrate having a job to do.

Today I can resent the mess the kids make,
OR
Give thanks I have a family.

Today I can whine about the housework,
OR
celebrate having a home.

Today I can cry over the people who don't care for me,
OR
Be happy loving and being loved by those who do.

I CHOOSE TO HAVE A GOOD DAY, TODAY!!!

TODAY, I CAN...

(Ralph Holt)

Surprise...Surprise!

EARLY IN 1995, on a rainy, cold nasty February day, a long black limousine traveling down the New Jersey expressway was forced to pull off to the side of the road with a flat tire. The limo driver dutifully got out to change the tire, only to discover that the spare tire was also flat. Before the uniformed driver could summon a road service, a man in a pickup truck pulled up behind the limo, stopped, got out and offered to help. Among the jumble of equipment in the back of his construction truck was an air tank.

The pickup driver quickly fixed the flat, aired it up and placed it back on the limo. As the job was finished, the rear window slid down and the truck driver was surprised to see Donald Trump sitting inside. "This was so very nice of you to stop and help," Trump said, "What can I do to thank you?"

The man thought for a moment and said, "Tomorrow is Valentine's Day. My wife would really get a kick out of receiving a dozen red roses from you."

Trump agreed, got the name and address and drove off with the fixed flat tire on his limo.

The next day, a floral messenger arrived at the home with a long box. When the surprised wife opened the box she found two dozen red roses and a note which read: "Happy Valentine's Day from a friend of your husband. (signed) DONALD TRUMP."

And at the bottom of the note there was a PS: "Thanks for helping us out. By the way, I paid off your home mortgage." (Ken Dolan, *Straight Talk on Your Money*, vol. 5, num. 5, pg. 1, adapted)

Yes...this is a true story! What a story of canceled debt! What an exciting way to be able to live...canceling debts of others. There's an even more exciting story about canceling a debt too large to pay. Jesus Christ came to live among us to be able to die for us in a sacrifice which canceled all the debts of past sins! Now...that's worth a celebration!

When we look at life…what does really matter? What really counts in life? Get to the essence of the matter. What matters most? It's a question that always seems to be hanging in the air. Christ died for our sins so that we could enjoy eternal life.

For I delivered to you first of all that which I also received:
that Christ died for our sins according to the Scriptures,
And that He was buried,
And that He rose again the third day according to the Scriptures…
(I Corinthians 15:3-4)

Theology

HAVE you ever attempted to explain God to your child or any other child? How does a child's young mind grasp the nature of God? Well… here is a very special explanation I discovered, written by an eight-year-old. It was an essay for his teacher. The young Danny Dutton writes the following:

"One of God's main jobs is making people. He makes these to put in place of the ones that die so there will be enough people to take care of things here on earth. He doesn't make grownups. Just babies. I think because they are smaller and easier to make. That way He doesn't have to take up His valuable time teaching them to talk and walk. He can just leave that up to the mothers and fathers. I think it works out pretty good.

"God's second most important job is listening to prayers. An awful lot of this goes on, as some people, like preachers and things, pray other times besides bedtime, and Grandpa and Grandma Dutton pray every time they eat except for snacks. God doesn't have time to listen to the radio or TV on account of this. As He hears everything, not only prayers, there must be a terrible lot of noise going on in His ears unless He has thought of a way to turn it off. I think we should all be a little quieter.

"God sees everything and hears everything and is everywhere. Which keeps Him pretty busy. So you shouldn't go wasting His time asking for things that aren't important or go over your parent's head and ask for something they said you couldn't have." (Calvinist Contact, from Men's Life, Oct. 11, 1985)

Pretty articulate for an eight-year-old, don't you agree? And yes, explaining God can be a tough assignment. When do we do it? How do we go about it? How often will we be called upon to explain? Also I understand that at age four they have all the questions and at fourteen they have all the answers. It does complicate things.

But the Bible gives us some very strong clues about knowing God and this first step is to begin with parents, "You shall love the LORD your God with all your heart, with all your soul, and with all your strength," (Deuteronomy 6:5). Then the concepts and precepts of God are to be taught "diligently to your children, and shall talk of them when you sit in your house, when you walk by the way, when you lie down, and when you rise up" (Verse 7). Set the example and share it with your kids.

A house is built of logs and stone,
Of tiles and posts and piers;
A home is built of loving deeds
That stand a thousand years.
(Victor Hugo)

"You shall walk in all the ways which the LORD your God has commanded you, that you may live and that it may be well with you, and that you may prolong your days in the land which you shall possess" (Deuteronomy 5:33).

A Mother's Love

This is a true story which took place in one of the Nazi concentration camps during World War II. (It's a story that I heard at a minister's conference.) The Rosenberg family had been imprisoned in a work camp where the gas ovens could be avoided as long as a person was able to work.

Grandpa Rosenberg and his wife, well into their eighties, barely survived the long hours, lack of decent food and miserable hygienic conditions. They were soon sent to their deaths.

The Solomon Rosenbergs had their two sons with them in the camp. The younger, David, was handicapped. Solomon had feared first for his parents, then for David, who surely would be the next victim.

Each morning the family separated for their work assignments. Each night they returned to huddle together in the barracks. Each day Solomon wondered if this would be the day that his wife or David would be taken. So as he entered the barracks at night, his eyes quickly sought out his family.

At last the night came that Solomon had feared. As he walked into the barracks he could see none of his family. He became frantic as he searched for their faces...then, he saw the figure of his oldest, Jacob, hunched over, weeping. Solomon hurried over, "Jacob, tell me it isn't so. Did they take David today?"

"Yes, Papa. Today they came to take David. They said he could no longer do his work," he said sadly.

"But, Mama, where is Mama? She is still strong. Surely they didn't take Mama, too?" he asked.

Jacob looked at his father through tear-filled eyes and said, "Papa, Papa. When they came to take David, he was afraid. And he cried. And so Mama said to David, 'Don't cry, David, I will go with you and hold you close.' So Mama went with him to the ovens so he wouldn't be afraid."

*God has promised to be with you, **Mother**, no matter what kind of days are ahead. He's promised never to leave or forsake you. In fact, He's written 365 "fear nots"! One for every day of this coming year!*

For He Himself has said, "I will never leave you nor forsake you."
So we may boldly say:
"The Lord is my helper;
I will not fear.
What can mankind do to me?"
(Hebrews 13:5b-6)

Attitude

THIS IS one of those wonderful, heart-warming stories about a husband who is going to ask for a raise. He told his wife that on this particular Friday he was going into the boss's office to request the raise which he felt was justly deserved. Naturally he was a bit nervous and apprehensive. Toward the end of the working day he finally mustered the courage to approach his boss with the request, which he had carefully rehearsed in his mind. The words must come out just right. To his very pleasant surprise, the employer readily agreed that, indeed, he was entitled to the requested increase in salary!

When he arrived home that evening he noticed the dining room table was set with their best dishes, candles were burning and a centerpiece was in place. His wife had prepared a festive, gourmet meal. He thought to himself, *"Perhaps someone at the office might have tipped her off that I did get the raise."* He went into the kitchen, and told her the good news. They hugged, they kissed, she said the kids were at Grandma's, then he sat down to his very favorite dinner. Beside his plate was a beautifully hand-lettered note from her which read: "Congratulations, darling! I knew you'd get the raise. These things will tell you how much I and the kids really love you!"

They enjoyed the meal together, they laughed, he shared the story with her, they celebrated and they planned! When she got up to bring the dessert, he noticed a second card fall from her pocket. He bent over, picked it up and read: "Don't worry about not getting the raise. You deserved it anyway! These things will tell you how much I and the kids really love you!"

What a delightful attitude! What an encourager she was! And she prepared for all possibilities!

Love is more than an emotion, it's an action directed to another person, motivated by our relationship to Jesus Christ, and is given freely without a personal reward in mind.

A word fitly spoken is like apples of gold in settings of silver. Like an earring of gold and an ornament of fine gold...
(Proverbs 25:11-12a)

Giving

MOTHER...do you ever have a difficult time thinking of what to give people for that "special" occasion? Events like birthdays, graduations, weddings, Christmas, friendship, illness or for anything else. This is not complete, but here's a suggested gift list of ten things to which you can refer when you are stumped. And best of all...you don't have to shop or wrap these in order to give them:

1) The gift of a ***LISTENING EAR:*** This is a gift you can give to most people...little or big. This is especially for those who might be living alone. When you do this, really, really listen. No interruptions, no daydreaming, no planning your clever responses. Just listen!

2) The gift of ***GENUINE AFFECTION:*** Determine to be generous with your hugs, kisses and gentle touches. Let these small actions convey the love that is inside of you. This is especially true when around little ones.

3) The gift of a ***CAREFULLY WRITTEN NOTE:*** Make it as simple as an "I love you" to a personally composed sonnet. Put these nuggets where they might surprise your target. These have the greatest impact when least expected.

4) The gift of ***LAUGHTER:*** How about sharing a cartoon? Cut it out and send it, fax it or e-mail it. Keep that clever article. Use it later. Share a good joke. Select a humorous card. This gift says to someone, "I love to laugh with you." Very therapeutic for life and relationships.

5) The gift of an ***HONEST COMPLIMENT:*** A simple "You look good in red" or "I like your wonderful attitude" or "Honey, thanks for the paycheck every week." These are great spirit lifters to people in your life who may think they are being taken for granted.

6) The gift of a ***FAVOR:*** How about pitching in and helping with the spring clean-ing, baby sitting, running errands, cleaning out the garage, fixing a meal when someone is sick, etc. It's easy…just think of what you would appreciate if it were done for you.

7) The gift of ***BEING LEFT ALONE:*** Not everyone will need this gift. But there are often times when they or we may want nothing more than to be left alone…some quiet and solitude. Become sensitive to those needy times and give this gift without being asked.

8) The gift of a ***CHEERFUL DISPOSITION:*** How about trying to be more cheer-ful around those who might need it most. Maybe their day hasn't gone well. Maybe they are simply in need of having their spirit lifted. Be sensitive about this as well.

9) The gift of a ***GAME:*** Offer to play with your child, neighbors, husband, or a friend their favorite game. This may not be your thing but it just may be theirs. Be happy when participating. Be patient. Even if you lose you'll be a winner!

10) The gift of ***PRAYER:*** Pray for those on your gift lists and let them know you are praying for them. Tell them, write a note to this effect. Praying for anoth-er is a very wonderful way of saying "You are so special to me that I'll talk to God about you and on your behalf."

The Mother's Day Hymn

The Reverend Barry Bence of Canada writes:

"A strange thing happened to me when I became a father back in 1974. I also became a feminist. Having daughters who would one day make their way in a world which still shows remarkable insensitivity to women made me mad enough to try and change things.

"First off, I had and still have a lot of work to do in my own attitudes and conduct. But more recently, I was planning a worship service for a Sunday on which we read the Bible's account of the story of Ruth and Miriam, and also the story of Mary Magdalene and her discovery of the Risen Christ in the garden where He had been buried just a few days before. I looked through our church's hymnal to find a hymn that thanked God for all that our fore-mothers in the faith had given to us, and guess what, there really were none. So I sat down and wrote my own. For those musically inclined, this hymn is to the tune of *"A Mighty Fortress"* and any church who wishes to sing it in a service of worship is welcome to find the music and share."

And here are the words he wrote:

> *Praise God whose love shines warm and bright*
> *in every woman's caring,*
> *Whose heartbeat throbs for all the world*
> *in every woman's daring.*
> *Our mother, daughter, wife,*
> *are fountains of your life...*

In Christ our sisters, too,
*   are daughters unto you!*
Praise Christ once born of woman!

You made a man of earth's red clay
*   to tend and guard creation,*
The woman shaped that primal day
*   to bring forth earth's redemption!*
Our partner to life's end,
*   our Teacher, Lover, Friend,*
Bless all your daughters who,
*   like Mary, cradle you,*
Whose grace is of the Spirit.

But Ruth said:
"Entreat me not to leave you,
Or to turn back from following after you;
For wherever you go, I will go;
And wherever you lodge, I will lodge;
Your people shall be my people, And your God, my God.
Where you die, I will die, And there will I be buried.
The LORD do so to me, and more also,
If anything but death parts you and me."
(Ruth 1:16-17)

Truthfulness

THE LAST EMPEROR of the Chou Dynasty, who ruled about 2,000 years ago in China, had a very beautiful concubine named Baosi. The emperor loved her dearly but nothing he did could make her happy. She was sad all the time and had never smiled.

So the emperor finally offered a huge prize to anyone who could make her smile at least once. One of his court ministers suggested that the emperor might light up the alarm signal tower. According to tradition, the signal tower was used only to summon all the surrounding generals who supported the emperor to come to the capital with their armies in case of an attack. The suggestion was that when the generals came and found out that they had been tricked, their frustration might win a smile from Baosi.

This last emperor did light the signal tower. The generals and their armies came. Baosi saw the generals and armies leave in frustration and she was amused. It was the first time the emperor had seen her smile and laugh.

The enemies of the country heard about this incident and took advantage of the false signal assuming that the armies would not come for rescue again. Therefore the emperor was killed and the dynasty ended. Now, the Chinese have a saying to describe the beauty of a lady as, "Beauty that might cost a country."

Immediately this story brings to mind another about the people who cried "wolf" too often. Truthfulness is a trust which, when abused, cannot easily be restored. Motherhood is based on truthfulness when dealing with the sensitive lives of little people who are naturally trusting until or unless they, by example are taught otherwise. What a responsibility!

There is a story about a former President, Grover Cleveland, whose mother insisted on total truthfulness at all times. She modeled it, she taught it and she expected it of him. Did he pass the test? As a boy he insisted upon returning the egg that a neighbor's hen daily laid on the Cleveland side of the fence. Early on he gave proof of the honesty that would later mark him as a man and a future President.

He shall cover you with His feathers,
And under His wings you shall take refuge;
His truth shall be your shield and buckler.
You shall not be afraid of the terror by night,
Nor of the arrow that flies by day...
(Psalm 91:5-6)

The remembrance

that my mother loved me
and that she dedicated me to mankind;
the remembrance
that it was her thought
and that it was the inspiration of her prayer
that I was to be set apart
not to be a great man myself,
but to be connected
with the welfare of the human race...
I have never lost the inspiration of it,
nor have I ceased to be thankful
to my mother,
and to reverence her,
that she had such a thought and wish
with regard to me.

(Henry Ward Beecher)

Rules for Being a Mother

BEFORE you became a mother you were a human. We commonly talk about human "beings" but a more fitting way to say it might be that we are all human "becomings"! Maybe we should think in terms of "rules for being human" as well as rules for being a mother. Here they are...if nothing else, perhaps they will provoke some thought:

You will receive a body: You may like it or hate it, the choice is up to you. It will be yours for the entire period of your life, therefore take good care of it.

You will learn life lessons: You are enrolled in a full-time informal school called "LIFE." Each day in this tough school you will have the opportunity to learn lessons. You may like the lessons or think they are irrelevant and choose to ignore them. Again it's your choice. No matter, keep on reading.

A lesson will be repeated until it is learned: A lesson will be presented to you in various forms until you have learned it. You cannot go on to the next lesson until you have learned the one at hand. When learned you can go on to the next one. However, you cannot choose the lessons you prefer.

Learning lessons will never end: There is no part of life that does not contain lessons. If you are alive...there are more lessons to be learned.

There is not a better "there" than a "here": When your "there" has become a "here" you will simply obtain another "there" that will, again, look better than the present "here."

Others in your life are merely mirrors of you: You cannot love or hate something about another person unless it reflects to you something you love or hate about yourself.

Unfortunately...you will most likely forget all of these lessons!

There's one sad truth in life I've found,
While journeying East to West,
The only folks we really wound
Are those we love the best.

We flatter those we scarcely know,
We please the fleeting guest,
And deal full many a thoughtless blow
To those who love us best.
(Author is Unknown)

Love suffers long and is kind; love does not envy; love does not parade itself, is not puffed up; does not behave rudely, does not seek its own, is not provoked, thinks no evil; does not rejoice in iniquity, but rejoices in the truth; bears all things, believes all things, hopes all things, endures all things.
LOVE NEVER FAILS…
(I Corinthians 13:4-8a)

"MADD" Gives New Meaning

On May 3, 1980, Cari Lightner's young life was tragically ended by a drunk driver! This unexpected and tragic event too quickly ended her life and forever changed the course of her mother's life.

In the midst of the sorrow and stress of losing a teen-aged daughter, Candy Lightner made a vow not to let this tragedy and others like it go unnoticed. Only four days following her daughter's death, Candy met with some of her friends to discuss what they could do to make an impact on drunken-driving fatalities. Her life took on a whole new meaning that day as "Mothers Against Drunk Driving" (MADD) was born!

Then...this handful of purpose-driven mothers grew to twenty as they demonstrated in California's capital city, Sacramento. From there they went on to Washington D.C., where more than 100 mothers marched in front of the White House. They were totally committed to reducing drunk-driving disasters. They were determined that someone had to listen and take action!

The efforts of this core group ultimately resulted in more than 360 chapters (and still growing) throughout the world, a national commission against drunk driving, and more than 400 new laws in fifty states which address drunk driving. In addition, young people also concerned about losing their friends formed "Students Against Drunk Driving" (SADD).

Amid the tears, cheers and jeers, Candy Lightner believed that people who cared enough about their purpose could have an impact on the world around them. And she is absolutely right! Candy turned personal disaster into a monumental achievement by setting her course and following it!

Purpose, or mission, is determined by the development of values, balance, ethics, humor, morality, and sensitivities. It manifests itself in the way we look at life.
(Luci Swindoll)

I do not count myself to have apprehended; but one thing I do, forgetting those things which are behind and reaching forward to those which are ahead, I press toward the goal for the prize of the upward call of God in Jesus Christ!
(Philippians 3:13-14)

If You Find Me

To Whom it may be of concern:

You must know that I am chronically human. If any of the following signs are observed in my character or actions, please know that I am **NOT** emotionally disturbed or dying:

1) If you find me stumbling and falling, I may just be trying something new for a change. I am learning!

2) If you find me sad it may be that I've just realized that I have been fooling myself and making the same stupid mistakes over and over again. I am exploring!

3) If you find me terribly frightened, I may just be in a brand new life situation. I am reaching out!

4) If you find me crying, it just may be because I attempted something and failed. I am trying!

5) If you find me very quiet and introspective, it may be that I am doing some serious thinking and planning. I will try again!

6) If you find me angry, I may have just discovered that I was not really trying or giving half an effort. I am in error!

7) If you find me with a strange little self-satisfied smile, I may have just discovered that I have everything I need for growing some more. I am knowing!

8) If you find me ecstatically happy, I may have finally succeeded in the task I set for myself. I am growing!

Once more, these are life signs of beings in my human nature. If prolonged absence of the above indicators is observed, do not perform an autopsy without first providing a fertile opportunity for my life to emerge!

(Adapted from *Personal Achievement Skills Learning*, Arkansas Rehabilitation Research & Training Center, University of Arkansas)

People are like stained glass windows. They sparkle and shine when the sun is out; but when the darkness sets in their true beauty is revealed only if there is a light within.

(Elizabeth Kubler-Ross)

For you were once in darkness, but now you are light in the Lord. Walk as children of light (for the fruit of the Spirit is in all goodness, righteousness, and truth).
(Ephesians 5:8-9)

How About This

Have you heard this story? Now it's supposed to be the truth because it made a Paul Harvey broadcast:

At breakfast one morning, a spouse said to her husband, "I bet you don't know what day this is."

"Of course I do," he answered as he made his way out the door giving hugs and kisses to the wife and kids on his way to the office. At about 10:00 am the doorbell rang. She opened the door and was handed a box containing a dozen long-stemmed red roses. At 1:00 pm, a foil wrapped, two-pound box of her favorite chocolates arrived. Later in the afternoon, a boutique delivered a beautiful new dress.

The lady couldn't wait for her husband to come home. "First the flowers, then the candy and then the dress!" she exclaimed.

He answered, "Just something for you on your special day."

"Yes," she explained, "I've never spent a more wonderful 'Gound-hog's Day' in my whole life! Thank you, dear!"

Okay...and while we're at it, how about the couple who were celebrating their 50th wedding anniversary? They were asked the secret of their marital bliss. "Well," drawled the old man, "the wife and I had an agreement when we first got married. The agreement was that when she was bothered about something, she would just tell me off, get it out of her system. And if I was mad at her about some-thing, I was to take a walk. I suppose you can attribute our marital success to the fact that she vented and got it out of her system and I lived predominantly an outdoor life."

Love is mature when a couple enjoys being together more than being with anyone else, although others are not excluded from their lives. They discover that each can even have a good time doing something together which neither would enjoy doing alone. When they are absent from each other, each is in the background of the other's thoughts.

(Dr. Henry Brandt)

Who can find a virtuous wife? For her worth is far above rubies. The heart of her husband safely trusts her: so he will have no lack of gain. She does him good and not evil all the days of her life.
(Proverbs 31:10-12)

Real Wealth

Hetty Green never made the headlines to applaud her life achievements. And it's very likely you have never heard of this mother. During her lifetime, she was one of the richest women in the world, if not the richest in her time. She reportedly maintained a balance of $31 million in one bank and upon her death left an estate valued at more than $95 million. Now that's when a dollar was a real dollar.

However, the desire for more wealth consumed her and her lifestyle earned her a listing in the *Guinness Book of World Records* as "the world's greatest miser" if not the meanest.

Her miserly lifestyle included living on cold oatmeal so she wouldn't have to pay for the heat. Her son was forced to have his leg amputated because she refused to pay for an operation which would have saved it. The cause of her death in 1916 was a convulsion prompted by an argument about the virtues of skim milk.

Hetty Green was rich…but lived an impoverished life. Although she lived, there was no life in her living.

One day a newspaper reporter found himself in the presence of the fabulously wealthy J. Paul Getty. In his best interviewer's voice he asked, "Mr. Getty, what is it that money cannot buy?"

Getty pondered a bit, then replied, "I don't think it can buy health and I don't think it can buy a good time. Some of the best times I have ever had didn't cost any money."

Mother…what are you teaching your children about wealth and happiness? Really, there is no happiness in wealth but there is lots of wealth in the experience of happiness.

May we never let the things we can't have, or don't have, or shouldn't have, spoil our enjoyment of the things we do have and can have. As we value our happiness, let us not forget it, for one of the greatest lessons in life is learning to be happy without the things we cannot or should not have.

(Richard L. Evans)

And He said to them, "Take heed and beware of covetousness, for one's life does not consist in the abundance of the things he possesses."
(Luke 12:15)

The Sounds of Mother's Day

On Mother's Day all over the country, grateful moms are pushed back into their pillows, the flower on their "bird-of-paradise" plant (which blooms every other year for 15 minutes) is snipped and put in a small glass and a strange assortment of food comes out of a kitchen destined to take the sight from a good eye.

A mixer whirs, out of control, then stops abruptly as a shrill little voice cries, "I'm telling!"

A dog barks and another little voice says, "Get his paws out of there. Mom has to eat that!"

Minutes pass and finally, "Dad! Where is the chili sauce?"

Then, "Don't you dare bleed on Mom's breakfast!"

The rest is a blur of banging doors, running water, rapid footsteps and a high pitched, "YOU started the fire! YOU put it out!"

The breakfast, when it arrives is fairly standard for mother's day: a water tumbler of juice, five pieces of black bacon that snap in half when you breath on them, a mound of eggs that would feed a Marine division and four pieces of cold burnt toast with no butter but covered in peanut butter.

The kids line up by the bed to watch you eat it and make wonderful remarks about it. From time to time they ask why you're not drinking your Kool-aid or touching the cantaloupe with black olives on top spelling "M-O-M."

Later in the day, after you have decided it's easier to move to a new house than clean the kitchen, you return to your bed where, if you're wise, you'll reflect on this day. For the first time, your children have given instead of received. They have offered you the greatest of all gifts which anyone can give: THEMSELVES!

There will be other Mother's Days and other gifts that will astound and amaze you. But not one of them will ever measure up to the sound of your children in the kitchen on that special Mother's Day whispering, "Don't you dare bleed on Mom's breakfast!"

Then He said to the disciple, "Behold, your mother!" And from that hour that disciple took her to his own home.
(John 19:27)

Lunch With God

Julie A. Manhan has written the following:

There was once a little boy who wanted to meet God. He knew it was a long trip to where God lived, so he packed his suitcase with "Twinkies" and a six-pack of root beer and he started his journey.

When he had gone about three blocks, he met an old woman. She was sitting in the park just staring at some pigeons. The boy sat down next to her and opened his suitcase. He was about to take a drink from his root beer when he noticed that the old lady looked hungry, so he offered her a "Twinkie." She gratefully accepted it and smiled at him. Her smile was so pretty that the boy wanted to see it again, so he offered her a root beer. Once again she smiled at him. The boy was delighted!

They sat there all afternoon eating and smiling, and never said a word. As it grew dark, the boy realized how tired he was and he got up to leave. But, before he had gone more than a few steps, he turned around, ran back to the old woman, and gave her a hug. She gave him her biggest smile ever.

When the boy opened the door to his own house a short time later, his mother was surprised by the look of joy on his face. She asked him, "What did you do today that made you so happy?"

He replied, "I had lunch with God." But before his mother could respond, he added, "You know what? She's got the most beautiful smile I've ever seen!"

Meanwhile…the old woman, also radiant with joy, returned to her humble home. Her son was stunned by the look of peace on her face and asked, "Mother, what did you do today that made you so happy?"

She replied, "I ate 'Twinkies' in the park with God." But before her son could respond, she added, "You know, he's much younger than I expected."

You don't get to choose how you're going to die. Or when. You only decide how you're going to live. Now!
(Joan Baez)

For to me, to live is Christ, and to die is gain. But if I live on in the flesh, this will mean fruit from my labor; yet what I shall choose I cannot tell. For I am hard pressed between the two, having a desire to depart and be with Christ, which is far better. Nevertheless to remain in the flesh is more needful for you.
(Philippians 1:21-24)

A Recipe for Mothers

Pre-heat the oven...check first for rubber balls or plastic ninja men or Barbie dolls or little cars which might have been lurking inside.

Clear the counter...of wooden blocks, hot-wheels cars, puzzle pieces or toy stoves.

Grease pan. Crack nuts. Measure flour...remove Jimmy's and Jean's hands from the flour.

Crack more nuts...to replace those which Jimmy and Jean have just eaten.

Sift flour, baking powder and salt...get broom and dustpan. Sweep up pieces of bowl which was knocked on the floor, accidentally, of course.

Find a second mixing bowl...answer ringing doorbell, then return to kitchen. Remove Jimmy's and Jean's hand from the bowl. Wash Jimmy and Jean. Answer phone. Remove about one-half inch of salt from greased pan. Call for Jimmy and Jean. Look for Jimmy and Jean.

Grease another pan...answer phone. Return to kitchen and find Jimmy and Jean. Remove their hands from bowl and greased pan. Remove layer of nuts from greased pan. Sternly turn to Jimmy and Jean who knock the second bowl off counter while attempting to get away. Wash kitchen floor, counter, cupboards, stove, dishes, utensils and walls. Search for Jimmy and Jean. Find Jimmy and Jean and sit with them to explain that you are not really that angry with them.

Final scene...CALL THE BAKERY and order a cake. Tuck Jimmy and Jean into bed for their naps.

Take two aspirin.

Lie down.

A CHILD'S VIEW OF LOVE:

Some children were asked, "What is love?"
One little girl answered, "Love is when your mommy
reads you a bedtime story. TRUE LOVE is when she
doesn't skip any pages."

And now abide faith, hope, love, these three; but the
greatest of these is love.
(I Corinthians 13:13)

The Face of God

Following the devastating earthquake that struck Ecuador in 1988, an Indianapolis newspaper sent John Jackson, a photographer, to cover the story for their readers. One thing touched him more than anything else...the human suffering which he saw everywhere. He wrote a poem which was published in the October 10, 1988 issue of **Monday Morning**. Here it is:

The line was long
But moving briskly
And in that line
At the very end
Stood a young girl
About twelve years of age.
She waited patiently as those
At the front of that long line
Received a little rice,
Some canned goods,
Or a little fruit.
Slowly but surely
She was getting closer
To the front of that line,
Closer to the food.
From time to time
She would glance
Across the street.
She did not notice
The growing concern
On the faces of those
Distributing the food.
The food was running out.
Their anxiety began to show,

But she did not notice.
Her attention seemed always
To focus on three figures
Under the trees across the street.
At long last she stepped forward
To get her food
But the only thing left
Was the lonely banana.
The workers were almost
Ashamed to tell her
That was all that was left.
She did not seem to mind
To get that solitary banana.
Quietly she took the precious gift
And ran across the street
Where three small children waited.
Perhaps her sisters
And a brother.
Very deliberately
She peeled the banana
And very carefully
Divided the banana
Into three equal parts,
Placing the precious food
In the eager hands
Of those three younger ones.
One for you, one for you.
She then sat down
And licked the inside
Of that banana peel.
In that moment I swear
I SAW THE FACE OF GOD!

(John Jackson, Monday Morning, Indianapolis, IN,   October 10, 1988)

Not a Single One

Little Chad was a quiet, shy, withdrawn little kid. One day he came home from school and told his mother he'd like to make a "valentine" for everyone in his class. Her heart sank. She thought, "I wish he wouldn't do that." Because she had watched the other children when they walked home from school. Her Chad was always alone and walked behind the others. Chad was never included. But he insisted, so she purchased paper, glue and crayons. Then for weeks, night after night, Chad painstakingly made 35 valentines, his expressions of love.

Valentine's Day dawned and Chad was beside himself with excitement. He carefully stacked them up, bagged them and bolted out the door. His mother decided to bake his favorite cookies and serve them nice and warm with a cool glass of milk, his "bestest" snack, when he came home from school. She just knew he would be disappointed and maybe that would ease the pain. It hurt to think that he would not get many valentines, maybe none at all.

That afternoon, cookies and milk ready, she heard the kids outside. She looked out the window and sure enough, the kids were laughing and having a good time. But as always, there was her Chad in the rear. He walked faster than usual. She fully expected him to burst into tears as soon as he got inside. His hands were empty, she noticed, and when the door opened she choked back her tears.

"I baked your favorite cookies and here's a glass of milk," she said. But he hardly heard her words…he just marched right on by, his face aglow… And all he could say was "Not a one! Not a one! Not a single one!" And…then he added, "I didn't forget a one, not a single one!"

Not until I became a mother did I understand how much my mother had sacrificed for me; not until I became a mother did I feel how hurt my mother was when I disobeyed; not until I became a mother did I know how proud my mother was when I achieved; not until I became a mother did I realize how much my mother loves me.
(Victoria Farnsworth)

And Adam called his wife's name EVE, because she was the mother of all living.
(Genesis 3:20)

A Hand To Hold

THE EVENTS OF SEPTEMBER 11, 2001 will forever be etched in the minds and hearts of Americans. It has changed us in ways we had never thought. Time has passed since this horrific terrorist attack but our minds are still haunted by those appalling images of exploding airliners, collapsing towers and mourning families. But out of the rubble of broken lives are coming many stories of special people and their acts of heroism. This is such a story about a wonderful mother.

None of Dora Menchaca's family or friends have to wonder how this 45-year-old clinical researcher from Santa Monica, California likely spent her last minutes of life aboard the ill-fated American Airlines Flight 77. She was a mother who was a toucher, a listener, a soother, a caring person, an exacting scientist. Her job was heading up a research team to get experimental drugs approved.

Menchaca was also know as the "proverbial therapist's couch." She was the person with whom others confided their troubles and secrets.

She was a relentless professional. It was she while working on a drug treatment for prostate cancer who willingly embarrassed her male colleagues by demanding to know if they had subjected themselves to the proper medical exams. It was she who prodded doctors who practiced in foreign countries to move much more quickly on their clinical trials.

Dora was the daughter of Mexican immigrants who left behind a husband, a 4-year-old son and an 18-year-old daughter. When her business meeting had been canceled, she hurried to catch an earlier flight home because she wanted extra time in the garden and with her family. Flight 77 was this choice…a flight which was re-routed into the Pentagon.

Mary Ann Foote, her fellow researcher at Amgen said, "She was the mother figure. I have no doubt that Dora had someone's hands in both of hers when the plane went down."

I think about the families, the children…I'm a loving guy. And I am also someone, however, who's got a job to do and I intend to do it. And this is a terrible moment, but this country will not relent until we have saved ourselves, and others, from the terrible tragedy that came upon America.
(George W. Bush, President)

Who shall separate us from the love of Christ? Shall tribulation, or distress, or persecution, or famine, or nakedness, or peril, or sword? Yet in all these things we are more than conquerors through Him who loved us.
For I am persuaded that neither death nor life, nor angels nor principalities nor powers, nor things present nor things to come, nor any other created thing, shall be able to separate us from the love of God which is in Christ Jesus our Lord!
(Romans 8:35, 37-39)

A Child is on Loan

"I'll lend you for a little time a child of mine," He said,
"For you to love the while he lives and mourn for when he's dead.
It may be six or seven years or twenty-two or three,
But will you, till I call him back, take care of him for me?
He'll bring his charms to gladden you, and should his stay be brief,
You'll have his lovely memories as solace for your grief.

"I cannot promise he will stay, since all from earth return,
But there are lessons taught down there I want this child to learn.
I've looked this wide world over in My search for teachers true,
And from the throngs that crowd life's lanes I have selected you;
Now will you give him all your love and not think the labor vain,
Nor hate Me when I come to call and take him back again?"

I fancied that I heard them say, "Dear Lord, Thy will be done,
For all the joy the child shall bring, the risk of grief we'll run.
We'll shelter him with tenderness, we'll love him while we may,
And for happiness we've known, forever grateful stay.
But should the angels call for him much sooner than we planned
We'll brave the bitter grief that comes and try to understand."

(The Author is unknown)

The Laurel Burch Story

Laurel Burch had the courage to be different, to dream and to create. She is the founder and maker of "The Spirit of Womankind" jewelry. Her journey may encourage the faint-hearted among us.

Laurel says: "When I was a girl I used to collect stones in bags. I'd put them in different arrangements and love them. When I was seven, I put on shows in my garage for the neighborhood kids. I'd collect money from them, then figure out what I was going to do.

"I ran away from home at fourteen and ended up in a Catholic boarding school. That summer, when the boarders went home, it was thirty nuns and me. I didn't have friends. I didn't have parents.

"For the longest time nobody validated what I was doing. I wound up in the Haight in 1966. I thanked the friends who sheltered me and my two babies with gifts of necklaces and earrings made of wire hammered into twists using the flat bottom of a frying pan I'd bought at the flea market.

"I thought having two kids 'stacked the deck' against me, but by combining Egyptian beads, Chinese coins and odds and ends from around the world, I could hold onto my inside self. I worked in a jewelry store for $1.25 an hour, of which fifty cents had to go for baby-sitting. I had no idea my own time had value and I sold my creations for $2.00 a pair.

"It might have gone on like that forever, but one day I walked into a Ghiradelli Square store owned by Lois Smith, wearing a necklace of metal and beads I'd made. She loved it and asked me to make and sell jewelry for her and other stores.

"At first my reputation grew by word of mouth. Then I went to New York and bumped into an old friend. She took one look at the jewelry on my neck (overlooking the baby strapped to my back) and said, 'Come on, we're going to *Vogue*.' The result was two pages in *Vogue* and three pages in *Harper's Bazaar*."

She learned to muster the courage to go on! And as they say, the rest is history! If she can...so can you.

You gain strength, courage and confidence by every experience in which you really stop to look fear in the face. You are able to say to yourself, "I lived through this horror. I can take the next thing that comes along." You must do the thing you think you cannot do.
                                                    (Eleanor Roosevelt)

I know how to be abased, and I know how to abound. Everywhere and in all things I have learned both to be full and to be hungry, both to abound and to suffer need.
I can do all things through Christ who strengthens me!
(Philippians 4:12-13)

Overcoming Adversity

Track star Wilma Rudolph won three gold medals in the 1960 Olympics but to get there she had to overcome enormous hurdles.

Wilma had been born prematurely and complications developed that led to contracting double pneumonia twice, as well as scarlet fever. A later bout with polio left her with a crooked leg and a foot twisted inward. As a result, Wilma spent most of her childhood in braces.

Wilma's adversity created a determined spirit. She wanted out of her braces and by age eleven, she began sneaking around without them. Finally she told her doctor what she had been doing and proved it to him by taking off her braces and walking around, demonstrating that she no longer needed them. The doctor gave her permission to go without "sometimes," which in Wilma's mind meant never again.

By age thirteen she made the basketball and track teams. Two years later, she was chosen to participate with the Tennessee State University "Tigerbelles" during the summer. A teammate interested her in pursing the Olympic team.

At age sixteen, Wilma reached the semifinals in the 200-meter dash at the 1956 Olympic games and won a bronze medal as a member of the women's 400-meter relay. But she wanted a gold and vowed to be back.

She entered a demanding training regimen along with paying her way through Tennessee State University and maintained the "B" average required to stay on the track team.

When the 1960 Olympics rolled around, Wilma Rudolph was ready! In three electrifying performances before eighty thousand enthusiastic fans she won three gold medals! She became the first American woman to win three gold medals in track and field!

It's doubtful that any other Olympic champion has overcome such crippling adversity as Wilma did! NOW…what about you? You, too, can overcome adversity to reach your goal!

You must do the best you can with what you have and what you are and who you have become. Blindness, pain, cancer, disability, rejection, or abuse couldn't destroy our heroes of adversity. Self-pity, worry, despair and hopelessness were eliminated from their thinking. They endured, overcame, excelled and triumphed. And you can, too!

(Isabel Moore)

Fear not, for I have redeemed you;
I have called you by your name;
You are Mine,
When you pass through the waters I will be with you;
When you walk through the fire,
you shall not be burned,
Nor shall the flame scorch you.
For I am the LORD your God…
(Isaiah 43:1b-3a)

Action

Lillian Katz is a lady of action and inspiration. Where she got this from we can only speculate. But her drive and desire have produced impressive results.

As a 24-year-old, pregnant with her first child, Lillian needed some way to increase the family's income. She used the $2,000 which had been saved from wedding gifts and purchased a few supplies. Next, she submitted an ad to Seventeen magazine promoting personalized handbags and belts. This was in 1951 and the thought of putting a person's initials on products was a revolutionary idea. The ad copy read, "Be the first to sport that personalized look."

The orders started coming in, business grew until today her mail-order catalog company is known world wide. Perhaps you have just received one of her catalogs recently. Her company name? "Lillian Vernon Corporation" with annual sales in the millions. She, of course, no longer fills orders at her kitchen table but employs more than 1,000 people who process the more than 30,000 weekly orders.

Action-oriented people realize that they who want milk should not sit in the middle of a pasture waiting for a cow to back up to them. Lillian Katz didn't wait around for someone to offer her the opportunity to increase her family income or hope she would win the lottery. She made action the breakfast of a champion!

It's interesting that the Bible never mentions the dreams, ideas or intentions of the apostles. But also consider that an entire book is specified as the "ACTS of the Apostles." It was the performance of these dedicated people that drew the attention of the Biblical writer. Their achievements can be attributed to dedication and action!

If it were easy it would have been done before!

(Jeanne Yaeger)

**I am the LORD your God,
Who teaches you to profit,
Who leads you by the way you
should go.
(Isaiah 48:17b)**

The Worth of a Hug

Kathleen Keating is the writer who introduced the world to the value of a hug. Her excellent book, *The Hug Therapy Book* (Comcare Publications), does a beautiful thing as it addresses the question: "What's so good about a hug?"

Keating answers: "Hugging is healthy; it helps the body's immunity system. It keeps you healthier, it cures depression, it reduces stress, it induces sleep, it's invigorating, it's rejuvenating, it has no unpleasant side effects and hugging is nothing less than a miracle drug. Hugging is all natural. It is organic, naturally sweet, has no pesticides, no preservatives, no artificial ingredients and is 100 percent wholesome. Hugging is practically perfect. There are no movable parts, no batteries to wear out, no periodic check-ups, low energy consumption, high energy yield, inflation-proof, non-fattening, no monthly payments, no insurance requirements, theft-proof, non-taxable, non-polluting and of course, fully returnable!"

Hugging is without a doubt one of the most naturally therapeutic actions in which we can engage. Kathleen Keating also said that for us to enjoy the maximum benefit of the hug…we should be hugged or give a hug at least twelve times per day. Maybe it's time to catch up on your quota beginning with right NOW!

Sometimes the messages we give and receive from others can be confusing and frustrating. For example, perhaps you are like Alice of *Alice in Wonderland* when the Duchess said to her, "Be what you would seem to be…or, if you'd like it put more simply…never imagine yourself not to be otherwise than what it might appear to others that what you were or might have been was not otherwise than what you had been would have appeared to them to be otherwise." (Huh?)

The giving of a hug sets the message straight! It's a simple and wonderful message which is given! Just do it!

This is a daily reminder
That I have made for me;
To make the most of life
And to be the best I can be.
To treat others with the respect
That I would like myself;
To face upcoming goals
Rather than put them on a shelf.
This is a daily reminder that
I have made for me.

(Amy Martinez)

Then little children were brought to Him that He might put His hands on them and pray, but the disciples rebuked them.
But Jesus said, "Let the little children come to Me, and do not forbid them; for of such is the kingdom of heaven."
And He laid His hands on them...
(Matthew 19:13-15a)

Ten Commandments for Mothers

Have you heard about the young man who wrote his first book? It was titled *Ten Commandments for Raising Kids*. He later married and became a first-time father, revising his book and re-titling it, *Ten Suggestions for Raising Kids*. Some time later, another child arrived, then a third and it was time to revise his book once more. This time the new title became *Ten Hints for Raising Kids*. Then another child arrived and he became a first-time grandparent, the final revision of his book was made with the title being, *Ten Things I Don't Know About Raising Kids*. Well… so much for the "commandment" type of advice. However, let's take a try at it any way. So here it is…**TEN COMMANDMENTS FOR MOTHERS:**

FIRST: My hands are small; please don't expect perfection whenever I make a bed, draw a picture or use a fork. My legs are short; slow down so I can keep up with you.

SECOND: My eyes have not seen the world as yours have; let me explore it safely, don't restrict me unnecessarily.

THIRD: Housework will always be there; I'm little only for a short time. Take time to explain things to me about this wonderful world and do so willingly.

FOURTH: My feelings are tender; don't nag me all day long (you would not want to be nagged because you are inquisitive). Treat me just like you would like to be treated.

FIFTH: I am a special gift from God; treasure me as God intended you to do. Hold me accountable for my actions, give me guidelines to live by and when disciplining, do it in a loving, kind way.

SIXTH: I do need your encouragement (but not your empty praise) to grow with balance. Go easy on the criticism; remember, please criticize the things I may do without attacking me.

SEVENTH: Give me the freedom to make some decisions about myself. Allow me to fail so that I can learn from my mistakes. If you do this, someday I will be prepared to make life decisions required of me.

EIGHTH: Don't do things over for me; that makes me feel as if my efforts are never good enough. I know it's hard, but don't compare me with my brother or sister, or cousin, or anybody else either.

NINTH: Don't be afraid to leave me for a weekend together. Kids also need vacations from parents and parents need vacations from kids. Besides, it's a great way to show us kids that your marriage is special.

TENTH: Take me to Sunday school and church regularly, setting a good example for me to follow. Remember that I like to learn more about God.

Raising kids is something like holding a wet bar of soap…grasp it too firmly and it squirts away. But to get the most out of that soap it needs water and a bit of scrubbing to make it effective. Raising good kids just doesn't happen.

Today's Bible verses (*The Ten Commandments*) should be read from Exodus 20:1-19. Develop the discipline of reading these original commandments periodically.

Secrets to Building Strong Families

Americans have been duped, again! We have been led to believe that home life is deteriorating at an alarming rate. The reason is the government's "National Center for Health Statistics" in 1981 said that one in every two marriages is ending in divorce. What happened? In 1981 there had been 2.4 million new marriages and 1.2 million divorces. Presto! They then announced that one in every two marriages is ending in divorce. DON'T YOU BELIEVE IT! This is another example of the statistical lie! In jumping to this conclusion…they completely overlooked the number of existing marriages.

"What was left out is that there were 54 million other marriages that are going on very nicely, thank you," so wrote the pollster, Louis Harris. Each year, ***ONLY TWO PERCENT*** (2%) of existing marriages will actually end in divorce, according to Harris!

"A number of academics made a sensational splash and the media got a lot of mileage out of it," said Harris, and "ever since then, an indelible message has been chorused in church pulpits, academic broadsides, and political prophecies of doom for the American family. Yet in reality, the American family is surviving under enormous pressure." Harris began questioning these statistics after polling 3,001 persons for a family survey. This study showed a "glowing picture of the American family."

Among the findings of this Harris poll were these: 85% of families have a happy marriage; 94% are highly satisfied with family relationships; 86% said they are happy with the support they receive from family members during a crisis and ***ONLY*** 20% said they are not happy with family life!

Harris called the one-to-two divorce marriage-ratio ***"one of the most specious pieces of statistical nonsense ever perpetrated in modern times!"***

***BECAUSE** she understood me better far than I myself could understand;*
Because her faith in me, like a guiding star, steadied my feet, and strengthened heart and hand.
Because her cheer and tender sympathy were strewn along the stony path she trod;
Because of her underlying love for me, I better comprehend the love of God.

(Author is unknown)

Now therefore, if you will indeed obey My voice and keep My
covenant, then you shall be a special treasure to Me
above all people; for all the earth is Mine!
(Exodus 19:5)

Secrets to Building Strong Families...

Nick Stinnett, professor of Human Development and Family Life at the University of Alabama, and **John DeFrain**, associate professor in the department of Human Development and the Family at the University of Nebraska, decided one of the reasons the media focus is on the negative side of family life is they have no studies on the positive side. They devised a program called the "Family Strengths Project." They placed a notice in 48 newspapers in 25 different states which said: "If you live in a strong family, please contact us. We know a lot about what makes families fail; we need to know more about what makes them succeed." More than 3,000 answers poured in. When tabulated, out of that response, they discovered six keys were mentioned over and over again. SO...WHAT ARE THEY?

First) COMMITMENT: This quality means trust! It's the act of pledging, it's a binding together. These people expected their families to last.

Second) TIME SPENT TOGETHER: What to do doesn't seem to be as important as just doing it. Even working together is as effective as playing or vacationing together. Just do it!

Third) GIVING HONEST APPRECIATION: One mother wrote, "Each night we go into the children's bedrooms and give each a big hug and kiss. Then we say, 'You are really good kids and we love you very much.' We think it's important to leave that message with them at the end of the day."

Fourth) DEVELOP GOOD COMMUNICATION: Here is the foundational bedrock principle of building any kind of lasting relationship. This doesn't just happen. It must be worked at.

Fifth) COPING SUCCESSFULLY WITH ANY CRISIS: Even good strong families have to deal with problems. The difference is that they have found a way to meet these life challenges.

Sixth) DEVELOP A SPIRITUAL WELLNESS: To those involved in taking the survey, this was the most surprising of all findings. "Spiritual wellness" was defined by strong families as a "caring center within each of us that promotes sharing, love and compassion for others." It's more than simply being a church going family...it's the dimension of expressing in daily living what they are preaching and teaching.

A healthy, strong, caring, loving family is the place we enter for comfort, development and regeneration. It's the place from which we can leave and be recharged for positive living!

**UNLESS the LORD builds the house,
they labor in vain who build it...
(Psalm 127:1a)**

The Last Word... Don't Quit!

A mother, wishing to encourage her young son's progress at the piano, bought tickets for a Paderewski performance. When the night arrived, they found their seats near the front of the concert hall and eyed the majestic, black Steinway piano waiting on stage. Soon the mother found a friend to talk with and without her knowing...the son slipped away from his seat and he began his exploring.

When eight o'clock arrived the house lights dimmed, the stage spotlights came on, the audience began to quiet and only then did they notice the little boy up on the bench! He was innocently picking out, "Twinkle, Twinkle, Little Star." His mother gasped as her hands flew to her mouth in surprised consternation.

But before she could begin to retrieve her son, the master appeared on stage, took in the innocent on his bench and quickly moved to the keyboard. He leaned down and whispered to the little boy, "Don't quit...keep playing." Then Paderewski reached down with his left hand and began filling in a bass part. Soon, his right arm reached around the other side, encircling the child, to add a running obbligato. Together, the old master and the young novice held the crowd mesmerized!

In our lives...unpolished as we may be, it is the Master who surrounds us and whispers in our ear, time and time again: "DON'T QUIT...KEEP PLAYING!" And as we do, He augments, supplements, supplies, nurtures and gives until a life of amazing beauty is created!

This is the wonderful possibility of a mother's life!

MOTHER...

I think it was a girlish hand,
Unlined, well-tended, when it held
At first, my clinging baby hand
In gentle grasps by love impelled.

I think it was a youthful face
That bent above me as I lay
Asleep, and bright the eyes that watched
My rest, in that forgotten day.

I think it was a slender form
That bore my weight on tiring arm,
And swift young feet that watched my steps
To guide them from the ways of harm.

But years and cares have changed that form
And face and hand; have streaked with gray
The hair; yet is the heart as full
Of love as in that other day.

(Author unknown)

And she has her reward; not fame, or baubles
bought in any mart,
But motherhood's brave crown, the love and
homage of her own child's heart.

(Author unknown)

If you enjoyed this book, you will also enjoy the companion book:
Moments For Fabulous Fathers

Or inquire about the best selling series:
Mini-Moments for Mothers
Mini-Moments for Fathers
Mini-Moments for Leaders
Mini-Moments for Christmas
Mini-Moments for Graduates
Mini-Moments with Angels

Available at bookstores nationwide or order from:
RoJon Inc., P.O. Box 3898, Springfield, MO 65808-3898